C000178815

TALK YOU RO

Rebecca Tantony

Edited by Jonathan Bentley–Smith
Illustrated by Anna Higgie

Burning Eye

Copyright © 2015 Rebecca Tantony

Illustrations Copyright © 2015 Anna Higgie

Layout and typesetting by Graeme Bateman

The author asserts the moral right under the Copyright, Designs and Patents Act 1988 to be identified as the author of this work.

All rights reserved. No part of this publication may be reproduced, stored in a retrieval system, or transmitted, in any form or by any means without the prior written consent of the author, nor be otherwise circulated in any form of binding or cover other than that in which it is published and without a similar condition being imposed on the subsequent purchaser.

This edition published by Burning Eye Books 2015

www.burningeye.co.uk
@burningeyebooks

Burning Eye Books
15 West Hill, Portishead, BS20 6LG
ISBN 978 1 90913 651 9

CONTENTS

5. Where We Were

7. The Orange Blossoms of Andalucía

13. Alone in India

18. Learning to Love Olives

21. What Women Want

25. Windmills

28. Remembering the Orange Groves

33. Michelle

36. Miguel

39. On 24th and Mission

42. Death Valley

45. This City Is A Garden

48. Maria

52. Kingdoms Built from Sand

56. Waiting for the End of the World to Come and Find Us

59. We Are Braver This Way

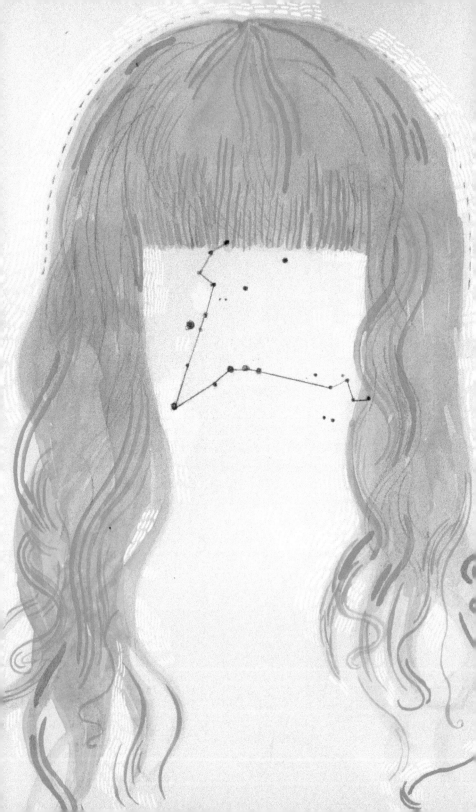

WHERE WE WERE

It was a Thursday afternoon. Her hair had been dyed bright red since the last time she'd seen him and walking towards the theatre she was concerned he'd no longer recognise her. That he only liked women who felt safe without colour and peroxide to hide behind. When she got there he was standing outside, smoking and fidgeting, looking from side to side and trying to find her.

'I'm here.'

'You're here.' He turned and his face broke into a love letter. 'You dyed your hair,' he said. She nodded and her eyes flitted from his pupils to the ground where she counted old cigarette butts, chewing-gum stains, a twenty-pence coin. 'Can I see it?'

As she pulled the hat from her head all possible outcomes jumped from her to him: he walked away; he asked her to dye it back; he pushed her over then kissed it better, pulling his lips across hers like a blanket.

'You look great.'

'You like it?'

'I like it.'

They walked to the waterfront, across cobbled alleyways and past expensive restaurants. Drank pints of beer in crowded bars. She was underage but never told him; being brave enough to add fake numbers to her seventeen years felt grown-up enough.

'Women don't normally drink pints,' he said, and she sipped her beer feeling both empowered and unsure about what women did and didn't do. I should go home, she wanted to say; instead her words turned into stories of her family, her ambitions, and her life so far.

'Do redheads have more fun?' he asked, and she laughed, throwing her head back, mouth so wide it seemed like her insides would climb out between her teeth and tongue.

'Let's find out.' She grabbed his hand and they left the bar, headed for the harbour and skipped along until they reached the edge. There, she stood on tiptoes swaying back and forth, looked at him with a smile and threw her hat into the dark water.

'What did you do that for?'

'I did that for me,' she said, before the wind set her hair free, spilling it across the sky.

THE ORANGE BLOSSOMS OF ANDALUCIA

When winter ended the wastelands of Andalucía exploded into colour and everything that had been bare was enriched by nature once again. The plants started living, yearning and pleading for light, and alongside the mountains shoots and stems broke through. Then there were the orange blossom trees. They grew everywhere, scattering reminders of their presence across Las Alpujarras, each blossom full of twisting veins, each leaf different from the next. For me they represented pure, unquestionable beauty and as the wind swept them through the sky, I would sit on the balcony and count them, thanking each one for spring.

Instead of breaking up we had moved to Spain.

'It's not us, you know,' he'd said. 'It's this city. Let's leave it behind and find something more together.' A week later we arrived in Capileira, welcomed in by bitter winds and grey skylines; the beginning of a long winter. For the next eight months we were surrounded by steep mountainsides, looking after a stone house on top of a hill; a place where we would chop wood and walk together. Where we would tend to the gardens and feed the dogs. Where we would separate ourselves from the familiar in order to become close again. Together, we would face the dark and find the sun.

Our first month was a cold November. Every night we went to bed at dusk, wearing thick fur coats that I'd found in the back of a wardrobe. I would lie there trying to find Sebastian's skin through the coarse hair and the smell of damp, feeling my way across his body like it was something foreign. 'You feel different here,' I whispered, and in the morning he would wake up, say that we were both different in Andalucía, like dreaming had brought him realisation.

The light only lasted for a few hours each day and in the darkness we took it all so much slower than we ever had before; roasting chunks of meat, brewing teas, letting apples soak and pickling time together. The longer we stayed the stronger we became, only it wasn't a strength found through togetherness, but by living as two independent people in search of who we could be this far from home.

Some days I'd slam the brakes on, extract memories and drop them in test tubes locked in three-inch-thick snow. We scratched our initials on tree bark so to remember how far we'd come. Our bones clicked, our eyes were small, we bled underwater like silent war wounds. On those days we caught only glimpses of each other. It wasn't that we were doing anything wrong; we just didn't know how to be in Andalucía. There was nothing left to hide behind yet we still couldn't absorb one another fully, instead appearing as apparitions to learn from. I was twenty-two and longed for the bassline of a nightclub or to see my friends' faces; Sebastian was ten years older and used to exploring the world alone. We were together in the stomach of beauty, and those winter months only brought unbearable loneliness for us both.

Opposite our house was a Buddhist monastery. Some days when the mist was particularly heavy it was hidden, then a day or so later it would reappear, a body of calm amidst all the confusion we were creating inside the big stone house. The hours were long; time seemed to have an entirely different meaning in Andalucía. The nearest village sold rugs and hams and little else; the nearest town was an hour away. We'd been left the phone numbers of people who lived close by but I never felt able to call; they were different somehow, they'd learned to live according to the seasons, they'd found peace in the silence. I felt so very unsure next to them all.

During that winter I became fascinated with everyone I could no longer see: my friends, family and colleagues, all of whom I missed now I was so far away from home. With this came a want to understand the intricacies of Sebastian and me. How could we relate to each other in the moment when there was a whole history between us?

Having promised myself that I would understand everything much better by the time I returned home, I spent hours reading. I discovered shamans through the voices of anthropologists; they were seekers like us who listened to the wind sifting through grains of sand and heard answers within it. I learnt of Native American rituals, ceremonies full of smoke and sweat, hanging hooks from chests and sick buckets full of magic leaves. I climbed mountains with these books in hand, the fresh air stinging the back of my throat like cheap tobacco. I sat cross-legged under waterfalls, trying to banish my thoughts to somewhere sacred. Though it never worked and instead I learnt that my mind was uncontrollable, so I stopped trying to fight it. I went on long walks. Huddled under pine trees. Breathed the smell of forest mushrooms and watched the world grow from a place of wonder. Throughout the enduring loneliness I experienced such intense explosions of clarity that little by little I learnt what it meant to feel surrounded by something.

When spring arrived we took to driving into Órgiva. As we sped along the windy Spanish foothills, I would sit in the passenger seat, counting all the orange blossom trees I saw on that hour-long journey.

'You're miles away from here,' Sebastian told me.

'Do you think there's a god who made all this?'

'No, I don't think a god made it. But I know why you ask. It's because it's hard to understand how somewhere like this could be so perfect.' And he looked both heavy and hopeful all at once.

On one of my lone explorations I read how an anthropologist living with the Yanomami tribe in Venezuela had wanted to start all her relationships again so she could relate in the moment rather than from memory. She raked through her past, finding every person she'd ever encountered in order to let them go again. Immediately, I pulled out my notebook and began writing down the names of everyone I had known, not because I wanted to forget them, but because I wanted to see them again, without marks, without having to look at them through an old frame.

It took four days of endless, frantic writing. I scrawled down the names of children I'd known in primary school, the names of people I couldn't remember anything else about. I wrote down my parents, friends of my parents, cousins, aunts, childhood playmates, lovers, boyfriends, teachers, housemates, co-workers, the woman who served me coffee every morning, the man behind the counter at the post office, my dance teachers, the boy next door who played basketball. I wrote them all down, and after I'd finished writing, I climbed to the top of the hill behind our house and burnt the paper beneath the sun's glare. Then I stood as still as the mountains, watching everyone I had ever known turn to ash. Realising I never needed to turn a past into a future in order to love someone now. Watching the wind and the orange blossoms carry them somewhere I had yet to discover.

White noise speaks sound; as kettle fish swim in swarms and the sun knows no bounds, our mouths conquer this silence. There is only love here. We find togetherness in language, a bravery in growing old, tiny ideas explode like supernovas, we orbit ourselves, always returning back to forever.

ALONE IN INDIA

The first time I tried to find God was in India. I looked for him in temples, behind stone pillars and above archways. I looked in the laughter lines that drew back the eyes of the sadhus, and I listened for him in the barefoot running of Indian children. I was sure that I would find his voice carried in the morning bhajans or his face hidden behind the four-armed statue of Krishna.

My friends weren't as eager as I was. Whilst I searched they drove away on Vespas rented for five rupees a day, whipping through dirt tracks and over skinny roads while the sun painted colours on their skin.

'Think you will have discovered him come lunch time?' they'd joke. 'It's just, we're not sure there's enough rice to go around.' And I remember laughing with them, kissing cheeks goodbye as they revved their engines, feeling jealous that I couldn't ride off and leave this aching behind me.

We spent six months in India. Started in the Himalayas where I watched Buddhists sitting peacefully with all the emotions that kept my friends and me constantly moving. We travelled through Delhi and headed south, every passing mile seeming to bring me closer to what I thought God might be.

In Varanasi I would walk down to the ghats of the river where the Ganga spat itself up against the banks. Standing on the wooden blocks, I'd watch people huddled together by the water. Most days there would be a funeral; bodies burnt on top of wood piles, black feet sticking out from under bundles of kindling and the smell of decay leaking into the city. Death was everywhere and within its tiny alleyways and residents, Varanasi spoke boldly about mortality.

One morning a woman, who was staying at the same guesthouse as me, went out on a boat that toured the waters. She told me that evening that she'd seen the body of a baby float past her, its tiny fingers reaching out of the water, its eyes open and staring up at the sky. I looked at her uncomfortably. This was where a dead body should be, the owner of the guesthouse told us, scattered amongst all the plastic bottles and old clothes, in the heart of India; the gateway to the next life.

Even though I knew I had to face it, I struggled with how open it all was. I would stare down from the top of the banks, awkward and unsure, as death happened around me. One afternoon, I was sitting there, scribbling in a notebook, when a group of boys approached me.

'What you writing about?' one of them asked, leaning over and pulling at my pen.

I wasn't sure how to respond. They were no older than eight and perhaps too young, I thought, for me to mention death.

'I'm writing about the funerals.'

They nodded.

'What about them?' they asked in perfect English.

'Just what's going on down there,' I said.

'What's going on?' one of them questioned.

Behind me I could hear women wailing, crying out for the loss of the ones they loved. I could hear the crackle and pop of burning pyres.

'We don't have this where I'm from. It's very open here.'

They were getting impatient with my slowness; fidgeting and looking around for other people to talk with.

'Does it frighten you?' I asked, and their smiles broadened.

'Why would it frighten us?'

The boy who had just spoken stared at me and shrugged as I became suddenly embarrassed at how much I had to learn from them. He said,

'Death is going to happen; why try and write it away?'

In the south of India coconuts sprang from trees as urgently as new leaves. The beaches cradled bleached sand and the sun was fierce. We travelled there just after I met the three boys; my conversation with them had stirred a desire in me that I wanted to understand. For a week we settled in Hampi as I tried to process all I had seen and learned so far. We were in a magnificent place, littered with ruins and exotic animals; while elephants plodded around, painted in bright colours, volatile monkeys scampered over rooftops.

In the centre of the town sat an old temple and on arrival I arranged to meet the sadhu who ran it. He was a holy man with a long, thin moustache and quiet eyes. I didn't know what to wear for our meeting. All my shorts seemed too tight and my T-shirts too low and I flung my clothes around the small room of our guesthouse in desperation.

'You need a sari,' my friend told me, pulling a bright yellow bed sheet from her single bed. We fell about laughing as she draped the sheet across my body, wrapped it around and held it in place with hair clips and safety pins. 'Perfect,' she said.

The sadhu was drinking chai under the shade of a coconut tree when I found him. I introduced myself with an open palm and we decided to walk together through the ruins of the old temples.

'What can I help you with exactly?' he asked, and I stuttered, still unsure about how to put what I wanted into words.

'I'm just curious, I think. I want to know more about your beliefs and why you trust them.'

He laughed. 'Are you religious?' As he said those words I felt the same sense that I had carried as a child, the feeling of never really belonging to something, but believing that I should.

'My dad's a Christian,' I offered, hoping he wouldn't mind that so much. 'My mum doesn't believe in a religion, but I know she thinks there's more than the ordinary. Like me, I guess.'

He nodded.

'I thought I might be able to find it here, a bit of what you've got. Some meaning to it all.'

He turned towards me. The sun shone behind him; licks of orange quivered over his shoulders.

'God means nothing unless you feel it here' – he slapped his stomach – 'and here' – and punched his chest before turning away. I watched as he tilted his face up towards the sun, closing his eyes as he did so. I turned and looked there too, hoping to see what had brought the expression which he carried so triumphantly. Yet even though we were staring up at the same space, sharing the same moment, we were experiencing different things that day. We were two types of typewriter text on blank backgrounds, meeting in between the brow of my doubt and his conviction. Speaking only in truth, swapping our questions for doors, an open ending, another room. My mind wandered. *As long as there's sun I will see you, God, because embryos form in war zones and penguins protect all of their colony. Because sometimes condoms split for a reason and heavy rain sounds like palms slapping drum skins.'* My heart thumped faster and my stomach turned. I watched a flock of birds dart through one another like threads through needles, moving together in a clump then splitting apart to fly the horizon alone. I watched the blue of the sky and the yellow of the sun. I watched nature standing for all I had been searching for and as the sadhu stared at the same spot and only saw God, I found everything.

In Athens it seemed to rain trombones and possibility, so everyone was dodging the inevitable yet there was always a chance of escape. We never got hit by music although I found you wounded by love, you said, spat out of a cannon and doubled over like a problem, short of breath and wondering, is this how it feels to finally fall for someone.

LEARNING TO LOVE OLIVES

'I'm sure you'll learn to love olives,' he says.

'I won't.'

'Yeah, I think you will, and anchovies and brie. I used to hate them too, but now it's like eating something holy.' His eyes look like they've been set alight, like there's a burning inside his pupils.

'They make me feel sick.'

'But your taste buds change every three months or so,' he says.

'Well, in three months or so, I might change whose tongue I want to put into my mouth.'

She says this because she feels intimidated. He's clever, he knows about human biology and what she will eat long before she does. And he's been proved right before, she's found herself learning to love things she'd thought she never would: the feel of his hands brushing her skin when she tries to fall asleep, the cigarette papers left scattered across her bedroom floor, the way he cares for his music collection as if he were the father of a thousand vulnerable children. Now he looks like he's been shot by her words. He's bent over, back arched and stomach collapsed in on itself, hands pressed against his heart. He sighs like he's damaged goods and she plans all the ways to say that she really does care, but finds you can't just stick words together and expect to make pretty. So she reaches out her hand to him and he catches it securely in his own.

She spends dusk making him laugh. They smoke cigarettes together and share words like kids at a carnival who swap gunshots for soft toys. Later in the evening she comes downstairs to find beer for them both. Having grabbed two cans she turns to head back, but then stops when she notices the bowl of olives sitting on the kitchen counter. As no one's around she thinks she'll try one again. She reaches out to the bowl, bravely sorting through the contents like it's a book full of important lessons, pages that hold the future in them. Awkwardly, she places one inside her mouth and even before it's reached the back of her throat she tastes the flavour of it. Something unusual and different. Her tongue seems to want to say there's so much more to find inside herself, there's a compass pointing in all directions and she sees in the same moment of separation, plugs fit sockets, fingers entwine and darkness reveals daylight.

So she swallows the olive. It's a strange fruit with a skin she's desperate to feel comfortable removing and a core she's determined to learn how to love.

Cartwheel over my mouth. Split teeth and tongue into a centrefold. I'm already a part of you, already declaring time to think it through, already saying that your body is autumn, bright lights and wet leaves, forgive yourself please, before the rain comes in thick. Outside women pull their legs apart for cigarettes; inside, I won't take anything less than all of you.

WHAT WOMEN WANT

We were both eleven.
I didn't yet know what it was to be heavy with heartache.
My lips were not ready to carry the sound of his name across oceans,
up mountains, within the sentiments of poems.
My stomach didn't twist yet,
didn't risk kicking my ribs yet
at the sight of him.
We were both eleven.

He didn't understand how the profundity of love feels,
he wasn't fascinated by females, but by the taste of Indian cooking.
When the teachers weren't looking he'd graffiti ancient languages on table tops,
أرى الحقيقة كما الذهبي
because he wanted to speak in secrets.

We were both eleven and we were kissing,
because that's what our friends had dared us to do,
so the river, the crickets, his breath hole punching the air in two
became one.
His tongue was a washing machine.
My hands didn't know where to go,
so I held him like I was shifting a wardrobe that contained
nothing
but shelves of
high hopes and low self-esteem.
We were all teeth and heartbeats and spit
during our first ever kiss.

After this, he never talked to me again.
We used to play hide and seek together,
running into the unknown blindly;
he once made me feel that life was about him finding me.
Yet I watched him leave that river,
seemingly unsure of what women wanted him to be.

Sixteen years have since passed.
In the meantime,
I've realised that I never needed a man to find me,
yet I have found myself a man worth learning.

WHAT WOMEN WANT

It is late night
and as stars are spat out of the black,
our hands collapse on each other's chests
and I cross myself over every single part of you that's left.
I draw equations across your skin,
adding and taking away everything we have ever found and lost together
and I turn to you and say,
sometimes I want to put exit signs above entrances because I'm afraid of leaving.
And sometimes, I say, I'm still caught up in the memory of my first kiss going,
of his zipped lips and cheeks blushing
the colours of bleeding suns and blood oranges.
Sometimes, I want to write you a list, scratched on the back of your heart
just in case you ever need to know
what women really want.

Number three goes,
It doesn't matter if you drive a fast car.
What matters is we feel like we're going forward together,
that we move each other to a place beyond stop signs and breakdowns.

Number two goes,
You don't have to be made of muscle,
your penis doesn't need to be of colossal proportions,
your strength isn't measured by how many weights you hold,
just carry your head high in adversity,
let your eyes burn like forest fires,
let the wrinkles of your face read like the details of underground train maps
and your skin smell like adventure.

WHAT WOMEN WANT

Number one goes,
Girls and boys, we aren't that different,
we were all born blue.
And what women really want is only ever all of you.
So let yourself meow and crawl as well as roar and soar,
show us weak and afraid and strong and secure.
Stumble on words, cry when you need to,
feel awkward and nervous if that seems true.
Hold that heart in your hand,
unashamed to let us see
every single surge of life
that really makes it beat.

WINDMILLS

We got lost on the way to your mum's funeral. One minute we could see the cars we were meant to be following and the next they were gone. There were just empty roads, endless fields and the silence that surrounded us all, the hearts that kept rattling against our chests and the presence of death that screamed itself apparent. At first we blamed you – Mum, Thomas and I – not because we wanted to make you feel bad, but because we didn't know how to find our way out of the confusion. We were afraid of missing something. Afraid we wouldn't get to say goodbye properly. Afraid of our own tiny, little lives.

You turned around in a lay-by; a three-point manoeuvre in a tight country lane. I stuck my head out of the window, tasted freshly cut grass in the air as I guided you back. Mum tried calling family members but no one answered, so we drove until we reached a crossroads and sat in the car for a while, silent and concerned.

Then suddenly you spoke, your enthusiasm pulling us all out of the melancholia.

'It's left. It's definitely left. I can tell by how many windmills are stood in that field there.'

I don't think I ever understood you properly, until that moment, Dad, when I realised we were both watching the world rush past and remembering it all in images. Me going from familiar cities to foreign hideouts, you from seaside towns to flat villages. Yes, sometimes I didn't know where I was headed either, but I could always find my way back by remembering the landscapes, the people, the pictures of what I'd passed before.

At the crossroads we turned left. I looked at the top of your head as you drove, pretended to draw a helmet around you, one with unicorns and stars on it, something to protect you from the world. I thought about how much grief you must have been feeling, wondering what it was like, having both your parents die.

Sometimes, I have felt the loss of those I love too. Boyfriends who slipped through my arteries as we both buried our hearts somewhere safer for a while; friends who came and went like buses do. Were you sad then, as we drove through the Kent countryside, through the hop fields your grandparents used to sit in? It was a black morning, yes, but in that darkness you still spotted those windmills, the ones that would guide us back to everyone we love.

'We're nearly there,' Mum said, and we all cheered, not in celebration but because we had all made it this far, driving back on ourselves, from times alone to times where we were brought together again, like curtains drawn apart then drawn across once more. We approached the church, and you laughed, because we understood how you see the world, and I smiled because I finally had someone to count the windmills with.

REMEMBERING THE ORANGE GROVES

I wondered if I would ever know the curves of your bones, Nicosia, the enamel of your wisdom teeth. I clawed at the space where mouths met, sliding my tongue across your jagged cliff edges, so sheer that I fell off daily. You were the last separated city on Earth. Like an angry bull fight, there was a divide between your north and south, between Islamic and Greek Orthodox. I'd travelled from Paphos, leaving buckets of red wine and swimming pools behind me. People had warned me about you, Nicosia. They'd told me you were split by a barren wasteland where soldiers patrolled with heavy guns. They'd said it was a place where I needed to be careful, a place where no woman should travel alone. And yet, along your divide, I found unusual restaurants and clothes shops. I found colour and celebration steps away from the booths where guards waited hopefully. I breathed in your air, Nicosia, wrapped a green scarf round my scalp, and made my approach.

'Papers please.' The guard held out her tiny hands, took my passport and stamped it with the mark of a new territory. I walked through. On either side of the city the streets looked the same, but in the north they were enclosed by a castle wall, a magnificent statement of something ancient and ornate that seemed to protect everyone who walked within it. The air smelt of hot fruit, sweeter than the south, sugary pastries and cinnamon tea intoxicating the back of our throats. People weaved slowly in and out of traffic, men huddled outside cafés smoking and spitting together, women moved in packs. I approached two elderly ladies who pointed me towards the bus station, where I found a large group of men crammed into a tiny office.

Following their instructions, I found the bus and climbed aboard. The four-hour journey from Nicosia took me over sandy foothills and through winding roads that offered lonesome stone houses and little else. The bus divided flocks of chickens into hot, dry air and sped past orchards of olives; the colours of the sky and the branches of the trees meshed together, creating a mesmerising blur. Apart from the whir of the engine, it was silent. I never spoke to the other passengers and they never spoke to me, for speaking would confirm that we were different, that language separated us like the wasteland that separated the two sides of the city. Within the silence, we could be the same.

I arrived in Lefke hot and excited, left the bus and began walking around the village. I could have been anywhere. It was quiet, the midday sun was keeping the villagers inside, and other than two howling dogs there wasn't much else moving. The community was popular, people travelled across continents to be here, so I knew it would be worth finding. But they didn't know I was coming and I didn't know who to tell. Back home in Bristol, I had spent time with the Whirling Dervishes who spun in circles to connect with the universe and find answers. They were the ones who told me that if I really wanted to learn more about their ancient traditions, then I should go to Lefke. So I had, and after searching for ten minutes I found what I was looking for. The sign that read 'Naqshbandi Sufis' hung above a huge courtyard full of ivy that spread itself across ceilings and wrapped itself around pillars. In the middle of it all, ladies sat cross-legged on the ground, muttering and pulling prayer beads through their fingers.

'Hi, I'm here to meet Sheikh Mawlana,' I said.

Someone laughed. 'Good luck. He's ninety-two and hasn't left his bedroom in three weeks.'

They all cackled together. The lady who'd just spoken asked me to take a seat before hurrying off to the kitchen to find food that we could all share. The women asked me how long I was staying for, and when I told them it was just a night they shrieked with more laughter; one night would never guarantee a sighting of the sheikh, let alone a conversation with him.

I spent the day with the women of the community, about sixty of them in all. We sat in the mosque, ate in the courtyard and then walked over to the guesthouses, where, just before dusk had dragged itself across the remaining light, one of them rushed over to me.

'The sheikh is giving a talk at his brother's house, at the top of the hill; you must come,' and she pulled me towards the orange groves that smelt so sweet after the day's sun that they nearly choked me.

The sheikh was old. The years had spilt lines over his face; they creased and dented when he smiled and his thin lips cracked when he spoke. His tiny body was wrapped in green cloth that contrasted with his eyes, making them appear intensely alive. I watched how the other people reacted to his presence with fascination, feeling the electric air, hearing gasps of excitement. I sat at the back between two giddy women who fanned themselves with old newspapers while he softly spoke to us all. After the talk he requested to meet anyone who might be leaving the next morning, so I went forward. I was ushered into a tiny room and sat down opposite him. We began eating sweets together, both of us on the floor staring eye to eye and chewing on fake fried eggs and exploding sherbet.

'I'm not a Sufi,' I said, taking off the headscarf, 'but that doesn't mean I can't learn from you. I'm trying to understand what it is to be alive. I thought perhaps being here might help me answer that.'

He nodded slowly, eyeing me with intrigue. 'Me too,' he said. 'I have been trying to understand being alive so much that sometimes I've forgotten I was alive. Forgotten about the orange groves first thing in the morning, forgotten about my wife last thing at night. Forgotten that I am one of seven billion others.' He laughed loudly, then leant forward. 'One thing that makes you remember is knowing it won't last forever. I'm going to die soon and what an adventure that will be.'

That evening I received three marriage proposals. Women of the community who had heard how, by chance, I'd got to meet the sheikh, now wanted me to marry their sons.

'I don't think you would want me,' I told them. 'I'm not traditional enough.' I like to swear and watch David Lynch films, I really wanted to say.

On the way back from Northern Cyprus, through the border and over to the other side of Nicosia, I wondered how different my life would have been if I had said yes to the marriage proposals and stayed in Lefke. I pictured myself picking fruits from the trees that grew around the mosque, swallowing hot rice and flat breads whilst telling tales of Bristol and my life before. I had leant on this place for answers and forgot the outline of my own shadow, lost her somewhere between Nicosia and Paphos. I'd sent a recording of my heart across a wasteland; shoes off in the mosque, new start somewhere distant, my shadow blurring into all the others I have found.

Let's let go of maps pointing to lonely corners, I thought, and meet in the middle somewhere between our cities, holding on tight in case life forgets us, and remembering our dreams. Remembering the boys in Paphos who carry treasures in their chests, their faces like memories I long for even before they've finished being made. And remembering the girls of Nicosia, goddesses of the city, all red lips and brave ideas. Let us live on a legacy left from glory, our bodies the cathedrals we once prayed in and our hands the answers to love.

I returned south with the knowledge that the sacred could be found in everything I'd left behind, in the ordinary and the mundane. It was in the house parties back home, those modern-day temples where sermons were spoken through backchat and expensive words. It was everywhere, it had always been everywhere. I just hadn't noticed it before. Nicosia, you told me that we were separate, yet all I found was our unity, a reverence for our differences, and evidence of just how similar we are. I travelled across your borders and boundaries, through your very centre, Nicosia, if only to hear who I was, through someone else's story.

A derelict man, an abandoned hotel, I found you at sunrise and fell in love with a combination of body parts. Your teeth, your tongue, your heart, your lungs, your fingertips, your skin.

MICHELLE

The light morning drawl comes to us from a woman sitting in a wheelchair watching as San Francisco wanders past the comfort of her porch.

'Where y'all trying to get to?' she asks softly, her voice sounding like a bird song.

We probably look lost, an upside-down map in our hands, faces crumpled in confusion, eyes open to whatever the next moment might bring.

'To the famous street,' I say, and she smiles, all knowing.

We step closer to see her more clearly: caramel body draped in sequins, short-cropped hair, an unusual face.

'My name's Michelle,' she says, and we smile, introduce ourselves to her. 'You're English,' she calls out, clapping her hands together and blinking her eyes so emphatically that we can almost hear her lashes speak. 'I'll take you to that street, if you like. 'Cause you're foreigners here.'

'Isn't that out of your way?' I ask.

'Any way is my way.'

We start moving forward together, Michelle turning the spokes of her wheels with the flats of her hands, us placing our feet with a confidence that comes with finally knowing you're going the right way. As we go Michelle points to every shop we pass, tells us what they sell, the names of those who work there.

'They have tacos. This place old cameras. You eat meat? They have the best beef in all of the city. Body piercings. Kate's there. Frank's here. Irish beer. Hair extensions.'

'Have you lived here long?' I ask her.

'Going on thirty years.' She smiles proudly. 'I moved from the south. My father was a milkman and I went to college down there. Where I'm from, African-Americans didn't study back then.'

I wonder why she came here, just like I've wondered why we've come here. I want to know what draws us all into this version of America, so I ask.

'Everyone can belong here no matter who they are. I can be myself in San Francisco. My parents didn't want a son like me in a place like Illinois.'

Politely, we try to find evidence of Michelle's sentence. We see the stubble growing from her jawline and the Adam's apple that sticks out just below. Her muscular arms spin those wheels in furious circles as we hear her high-pitched voice and we watch the sun catching the sequins on her dress.

We keep walking as people rush past us. Drag queens with their hair piled as high as the hopes of revolutionaries. A man sweeping his fingers across another man's cheek, so intimately you can feel the heat rush into their faces. Ghetto blasters weigh heavy on shoulders, gold medallions and cigarette smoke. Tight pink dresses worn by ancient women. Young boys waiting to grow into something grander, tiny dreams everywhere, skating, spitting, and the fight to be heard. Alive and awake; silence belongs to the villages we have left behind, and now we listen to the sound a city makes when it speaks.

'You have arrived somewhere safe enough to contain you.' Michelle laughs, stopping and reaching her hands out towards the sign for Haight and Ashbury, her nails painted red, her fingers full of plastic rings.

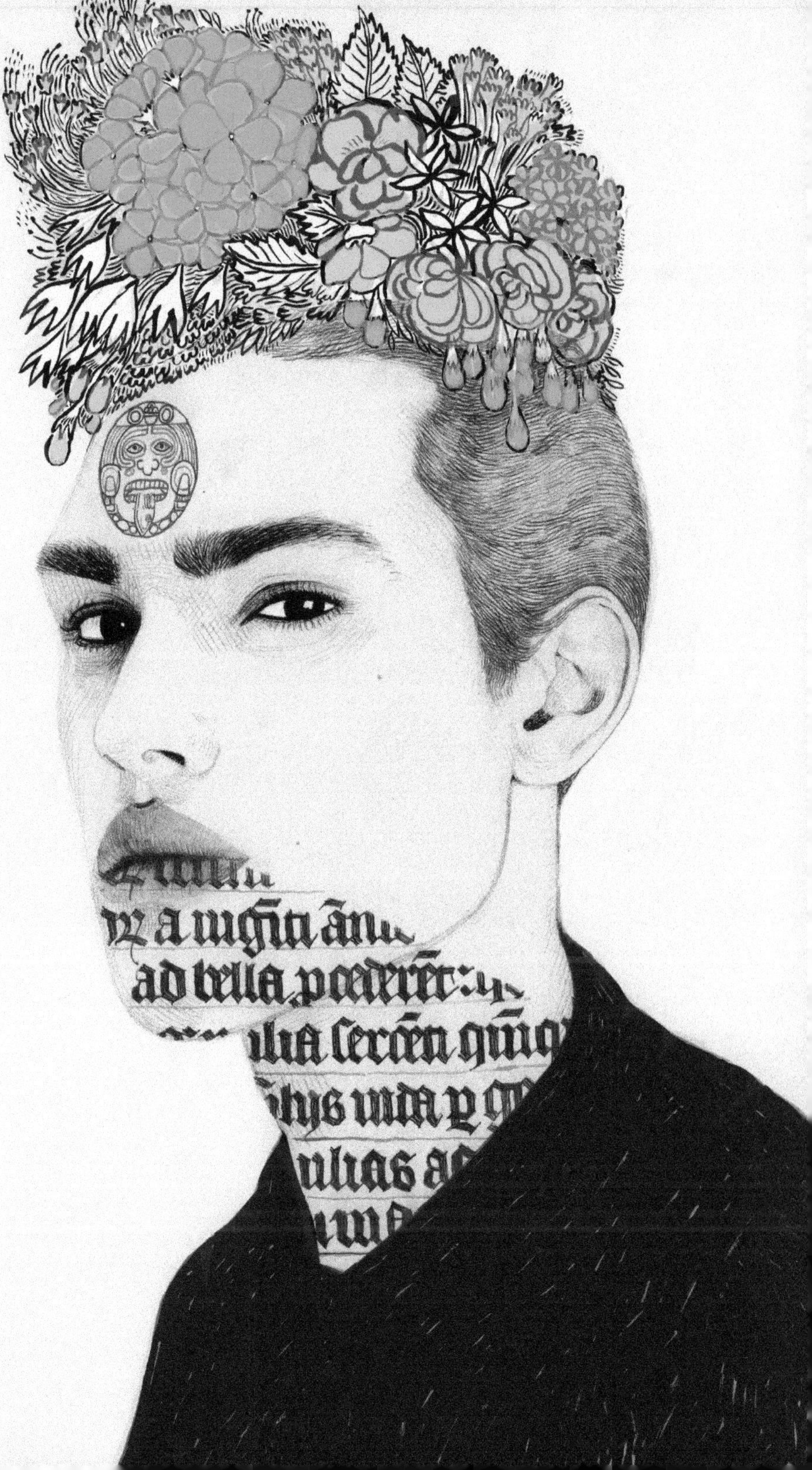

MIGUEL

I met a boy in San Francisco
whose silences spoke the volumes of encyclopaedias,
whose pupils shouted forever,
and whose mouth held so much possibility.

A boy who barely moved a muscle,
so quiet I thought he was mute
and while inside his stomach grew a town,
sat a city,
awaited a castle with a thousand empty rooms longing to be explored.
Outside, the world barked like hungry pit bulls
slobbering and shouting,
'Shhh.
Quietly… Miguel, don't say too much.'

Miguel.
He is fourteen years old,
in an inner-city high school,
in the heartbeat of the Mission District.
These Latin quarters speak in tongues.
In his palace,
a place where ghetto lingo spells out truths,
and youth speak differently here.

Miguel.
Dressed in a crushed velvet suit, teardrop tie.
An ancient disguised in high-tops, cap,
black slicked-back hair.
This half-American thing,
this Mexican king royally crowned.

Miguel.
Too afraid to say something?
Or too content to ever need to?
He's so peaceful between syllables, while I stuff words into the space we share,
eager for the next generation to speak of hope.
Shut-mouthed, clamped lips and quiet time.
We sit in the corridor together, and I tell him I'm leaving for Mexico soon,
I ask if there's anything I need to take with me
and he searches my face like a lighthouse scanning for something.

'Be. Open,' he says. 'It's not like it is here;
there you will find prayer in everything.
There are Mayan gods offering to wash your car with smiles that speak of heaven.
We are people who want to talk life.
Life and girls.
Girls, like my mother, who gave birth to me on the back of a bus
without drugs to numb the pain or a husband to feel it.
And my grandmother, who, in the five years since my grandfather died,
still tucks his memory in at night.
We are people who want to speak,' he says,
'of how to build the world's biggest gun.
Not to ever kill anyone.
Not to rip apart hearts, throw bones to earth,
pulp,
ash,
scatter,
sacrifice.
Not to hurt the human spirit.
But to point the trigger up towards the sky and fire a bullet at the sun.'

'But why?' I ask him.
'Because,' he replies,
'we all want to be heard by someone.'

ON 24TH AND MISSION

One third of the homeless population of America suffer from untreated psychiatric illnesses. One third of the homeless population of America are ex-war veterans. Half of them enjoy the way America sounds first thing in the morning when the sun is still breaking through and the cities are silent. One hundred and six have found kindness in the most unusual places. All have held something important somewhere along the way. In 2013, 6,436 people were homeless in San Francisco according to the city's Human Services Agency. I met one of them.

The world walked past us: young men with MacBooks, sharp fashion students, couples in matching tracksuits clutching each other's waists, a woman pushing a buggy filled with stuffed animals, a man in a wheelchair holding a football. And amongst them all, my hero stood still and spoke out.

He wasn't spitting bars loudly; he was whispering them. In the soft underbelly of the Mission District. In that land built from graffiti he stood outside the BART station with a mouth full of words. I was watching from the other side of the street, my hands clamped together as I tried to feel a connection to him through my heartbeat, trying desperately to understand what he had to say.

He was tall and thin with tight cornrows and a mouth as wide as forever. His words came frantically, rhythmic and soulful, as furious as a train in motion, but with a voice as light as flight feels. He spoke of the interconnectivity of all things existing, he said there was no separation between any of us, that the universe was enclosed within our bellies, sat there just waiting to be recognised. He talked about the places to find old bagels that still tasted fresh and the way his son looked at him six years ago. He talked about the death of his best friend and the crystal meth that lay scattered around her body like confetti at a wedding and how he saw in her last breath the freedom of going back to the person she had always been.

He was a messenger; I knew it. A warrior of language or a hero come to save us all. I stood still and listened close, trying to let his words find their way inside me, trying to let his experience collide with mine somewhere outside the BART station on 24th and Mission, and when it did, it was as if I was understanding language for the very first time.

The city got loud as evening spread across it. Lights and neon street signs flickered into life and I found myself thinking that I should buy my hero a coffee. There was a bar that I knew sold the best Colombian beans around and I thought that if we could go there together then maybe I could give him something in return.

I approached and asked.

'No,' he said, softly refusing, 'my place is here.'

I smiled and he smiled back, then he carried on talking to the city. Only there was more fight in his words this time; some came so fast that they made my skin burst, others were carried by a current so strong that they were impossible to hold on to.

'What's your name?' I asked, just as I was leaving. Just as it got too cold for me to stand out there any longer.

'I'm Hercules,' he said, and I nodded like I'd known all along.

As I walked away I carried his name with me. I took it into the station and onto the train to Oakland. As we rattled along the tracks, I plastered it across my heart, quietly muttering it over and over until it became the most heroic thing I had ever heard.

DEATH VALLEY

They'd been driving the spine of California. Past remote mailboxes and silent gas stations. Through endless stretches of desert; cracked dry earth and the arches of brick-red rocks. Over dams that separated lakes into swimming pools full of the deepest water and then into a ghost town where they stopped to take photographs of abandoned houses, old gas canisters and tiny baby shoes, breathing in the chloride until their heads hurt and the sun burnt down and their dry hands caught hold of each other. Amongst the rubble, the collapsed walls and emptiness, they found reminders of life: dishcloths, a hobby horse, cigarette packets. She looked around her and wondered what it took to leave it all behind like that, to get out of that endless desert and go in search of something more.

They returned to the van and continued driving, past chalky rock faces and cacti that looked like dancers caught in time. They weren't searching for anything in particular; they just knew they might never see any of this again. This vastness, this endless rock and egg-yolk yellow. Country music leaked from their muffled speakers, but all she could hear was the silence as they went from one empty town towards another.

Suddenly they saw something, a sign of life that started out as tiny black dot that stuck out of the gold sand before growing into the blue sky and becoming a gift shop. They found themselves inside it, buying postcards from a fifteen-year-old who refused to smile at them. She was everything they knew the teenagers back home to be, everything every girl had been at one point no matter where they'd come from. Bright lipstick covered her mouth and dry foundation caked her forehead. Her awkward eyes flitted from their faces and back down to the cash register.

'That's two dollars,' she mumbled, placing their postcards into a brown paper bag. They handed her a note and she frowned, told them how frustrating the new ones were because the paper stuck together.

'Must be a quiet place to live in,' they said, taking the change from her hand and feeling the dryness of desert embedded in it.

'Yeah, it's quiet, bit boring sometimes.' Her beautiful face cracked into a smile. 'But some days my friends and I get together and slide down sand dunes on mattresses.' Her features became solemn again.

One of them laughed. 'Sounds fun.'

'It's on those days, all of this becomes worth something,' she said, her face turning towards the desert.

They left the girl soon after that. He drove through the rest of Death Valley and she watched it all unfold through her window. They stopped a few more times: once to climb to the top of a sand dune, another to stare at the face of the Artist's Palette, and a third time by the side of a road. Mesmerised by the wonder that they were surrounded by, the reckless beauty that had passed them time and time again, she told him to slam on the brakes and they came to a halt. They sat for a while, just watching the empty desert pulsate around them.

'I want to stop looking for more,' she said, and so they climbed out of the van and stood together, remembering the girl and all the postcards they'd sent back home. Remembering this was what they had been dreaming of all along inside that tiny bedroom in Bristol. Remembering how sometimes, staying where you are and working with what you have can be the bravest thing to do.

THIS CITY IS A GARDEN

Sometimes, I'd want to leave behind
the way of the city;
go find silence by the edges of forests,
capture nature in my pockets,
etch its essence into poems.
Sometimes, I'd plant my feet on another type of ground,
bending down to gather seeds I'd later scatter across streets.
Remembering forget-me-nots might grow next to the overflow of bins,
trying to let some light in through the dirt of it all.

But sometimes there comes a moment when you just need to let go
and see this city is a garden; come discover my heart growing here.
There was never any need to leave, find life outside it.
We are a riverbed of roads,
streams of traffic leading us further into the unknown,

and I never wanted to be sure, you know.

We are here now,
between the flats that grow en masse like weeds buzzing
with a thousand species inside,
and the derelict buildings
where silence and solitude hide behind a forest of shops,
we're getting lost between carrier bags and street signs.

We are stood still now
in this landscape, fingers intertwined in the stomach of the city,
surrounded by wildflowers,
people who just grow where they're told.
Like the Colombian orchids who sip spiced rum in dimly lit bars
and the Iranian roses who gather where the English ones are,
on the corners where St Paul's and Stokes Croft collide,
two types told they could never grow side by side, becoming one.
At night, Spanish tulips perform songs to Cornish daffodils,
heads bent back singing soulfully, sweet southern sounds,
and Egyptian lotuses curl open with sunrise,
all wide-eyed; new mornings, days dawning,
as the Syrian jasmine traces pictures on his back
of the outline of their home.

THIS CITY IS A GARDEN

We are small flowers cracking concrete,
we're signals of survival, surprising us all
every time we think we couldn't get any further than before;
faces searching for the sun specks,
roots crawling under floorboards.

Sometimes, I'd want to leave behind
the way of the city;
go find silence by the edges of forests,
capture nature in my pockets,
etch its essence into poems.
But the breath of fresh air starts here,
at home.

We are rooted between the houses:
the beauty searched for found in the wrinkles of our two elderly neighbours,
their skin cyclical rings in oak trees,
and the growing we longed for seen in the decades
they have held one another's hearts,
and in the sweet smell
of her perfume, all fake lilac and violets,
and him and his cigars.

There's peace in the sometimes when we leave it all behind and stay as we are.
There's peace in the sometimes when we see there's so much more to find,
just here, in this garden, where beauty's of a different kind.

MARIA

Maria is both beautiful and intelligent. She speaks three languages: Spanish, English and French. She edits books on prisoners of war, paints her lips red and wears round black sunglasses that make her look like a 1930s film star. She has just spent a year in Paris, eating little but often, dreaming in French and remembering Mexico. It's her country after all, filled with her people, and that's why she has returned. Only the country she has returned to is different from the one she left behind. In the north a civil war is threatening to break out, thousands of people are dying. In the south there are people frightened of what's happening above them. Maria is frightened too. She doesn't go out at night; she stays in and works. She used to post updates on social network sites about her friends and their political activism, but then the government shut her account down.

Now sharing a rented apartment with her Parisian boyfriend, Maria's decided to make a go of it in spite of everything that's happening around her.

'Three friends were performing in the main plaza two weeks ago,' she tells us. 'They are actors, well-established actors. They were performing a play about civil rights when the police arrested them for disrupting the peace.' Her eyes are wide, big and brown; the colour of tree bark and the size of onion bulbs. When she talks you can see the panic that makes her want to hide and the hope that drives her on. You can see the gunshots and revolutions and the centuries of people wanting to make a difference. You can see a woman who has learnt three languages so she can understand the voices of those around her, so she can listen to how the world speaks.

In the kitchen the kettle whistles a high-pitched scream. We're boiling water because the bottles are empty and the stuff in the taps will make us ill. Her boyfriend starts pouring it into glasses and I wonder how much of this conversation he understands through her words and how much he feels in the pit of his stomach.

'They're facing thirty years in prison,' Maria says. 'Thirty years for acting in a play.' I stare back at her.

'I have to decide now what I do about it. Do I help them? Do I speak out or stay silent? I can risk my own life, that is my decision, but it's the lives of those around me I put at risk too.' She turns to the kitchen, to her boyfriend who is flipping tortes in the frying pan. The smell of cooking infiltrates the air; eggs tangled with peppers and onions, thick potatoes and chillies fried in oil. 'But what can I do? Can I stay quiet and be another one waiting for difference without doing anything to help it come?' She looks down at her hands, her long thin fingers; they tap the table as if playing the piano, the most sombre music ever made. I can't stop staring at her face; I look past the few lines of age, and the fewer lines of laughter. I look at her red lips, drawn downwards like an upside-down moon. Then I look around to the man she loves and I understand; she just wants to be able to offer a version of home that's good enough.

MARIA

After leaving Maria we travelled around Mexico for two months. I kept caution close to my chest as we continued on. Yet with every person I encountered I gave a little more of myself and bit by bit my guard fell apart, as if it had only ever been made from dust. I was opened up by the music played in tiny cafés and the houses painted brave colours. I was drawn in by the art that was for the cities and their streets, not just the galleries. I took in the bright-coloured fabrics, the shop front decorations, the beauty on the sides of buses. Maria and others like her crossed my mind often, those determined to keep exploding – the quiet ones, the outspoken ones, the ones who move across continents and return with stories of more, the ones who lead thousands into victory. In spite of the fear, in spite of how tiny they think they are, fighting from the ground up, to make a nest out of twigs again. I began to think as much of her hope as I had of her fear. I began to think of the warmth and the openness that keeps Mexico more honest than any other place I know.

Unplanned sleepovers and chip shops, stuffing my face into your mind, pulling apart time until it warps into this moment. This one we're growing into. Your body curving my body like the round edge of the Earth. An oven-cooked tongue, a 'no return' sticker on our worth. Like the war we fought. Like my patience. Like the breakfast in bed that never came. Like the feedback of warriors walking away.

KINGDOMS BUILT
FROM SAND

When the kingdom of Yugoslavia was at war with itself,
when bullets split organs and families became
scattered
fragments
of a
whole,
his Croatian father met his Serbian mother on a bridge
that joined their two countries together.
They hid in a safe house just below the gunshots,
learning the language of silence,
mouthing forgiveness to one another's skin,
looking past borders and discovering a universe
within the deep, dank pit of that place.
Love wasn't tired there,
wasn't fighting for liberation like it was outside.
It was full up and splitting atoms,
shooting out through the underbelly of this Earth.

His father had always ached to walk the spine of Dubrovnik.
'I want to shave my beard off,' he'd say, 'and let my mouth
taste unfamiliar things one day.'
His mother longed to close her eyes, imagining a different
future.
Neither settling for one another's dreams.

We all know love is sometimes letting go,
they had wanted to say,
but instead they spoke of whispering pines and stretches of sand.
Spoke of the silence that turned their countries into prisons,
and of how they would never run again from something built on chaos.
We were in Paris when he told me this story.
Told me that his parents had spent thirty-four years together, making two tiny boys
that grew into giants with brave eyes, before separating into two.

Just like a kingdom that proclaimed its independence.
Just like a kingdom that was fighting to be heard.

Back in England the sun shines hot, white light
while my mother and I sit beneath its glare.
I am drawing circles in the sand;
she is writing a letter to my father explaining that their marriage has ended.
She never signs her name,
he has heard it a thousand times already,
instead she just leaves a blank space,
a sign of where their futures can be found.
She tells him that their footsteps can be imprinted in different directions,
she knows that now,
knows that there is a world without each other to be discovered,
a bridge to meet in the middle of
and a safe house beneath its passing
that will remind them of home.

Perhaps this is the truest expression of love,
undefined by limitations, felt in the bones, transferred through our skin.
A love that doesn't speak of a future or a past,
but just proclaims how endless it always was.

Let's find one another there, in that open place,
crossing a bridge over into new lands.
From Croatia to Serbia. Paris to England.
Where the traffic rushes through our bodies,
and electrical storms flicker under our pulses.
Where our hearts are hot and heavy
with the weight of all this feeling.
Of all this coming together and leaving again.
Of all this love that knows
there isn't a kingdom big enough to contain it.

The world has ended, black floods colour, the moon cracks, we remember the sun.
He's still waiting for tomorrow, she's lost in today, bedrooms keep secrets, eyes tell truths.
I count sunrises so to remember my age, its rays warm the bones of our winters.
Our hands keep one another honest until the sky knows nothing of finish lines.

WAITING FOR THE END OF THE WORLD TO COME AND FIND US

Nicholas and I had landed amongst dead dogs strewn on the roadside and an orchestra of beeping cars. Amongst ten million people fighting their way through ten million people. We'd come to a place of lost languages, lost cultures; the descending steps of moon temples and the walkways of death. We were surrounded by warm people who drew our uncertainties away with their eyes, who made us feel unique. We saw Frida Kahlo's home, where she'd painted and fucked; her pain still in the air so heavy that it could suffocate us all. We fell into colour and passion. We collapsed under the hot dry sun. It was December 2012. We were in Mexico, waiting for the end of the world to come.

We travelled through back canals, past clucking hens and palm trees, past kingfishers and restaurants where loud, happy families spilt out through entrances. We clung onto each other, not knowing how to speak as well as we'd like to. The individual details of our lives were disappearing; we didn't have the capacity to tell anyone who we were and why we were there. We could no longer sell ourselves, charm others with our words. We were simply polite and humble, left only with the desire to give back to the place that was speaking for us.

In the evenings we dined in caves lit by thousands of candles, eating cheeses, beans, meats and fresh vegetables; drinking cinnamon rice as we watched traditional dancers move parts of their bodies that had long been redundant to us. We took in Oaxaca and its crafts, saw beautiful black-haired women sitting in huddles by the sides of thin roads, their old hands weaving brightly coloured threads. Ornate cathedrals stood proud over market plazas where stalls sold wooden animals painted ocean blue and neon pink. We counted down how long we had left until the world ended – just five days – and so we headed for Palenque, for tropical jungle, slick black jaguars and spiders with the faces of children.

At times, that rainforest felt to me like a womb might have done, an all-forgiving mother tongue. Its ground was full of skinny branches that cracked underfoot in code and its soil spoke in sonnets. It was a hold-your-arms-open, rich, thick place. All luscious. All giving. A place that you could surrender yourself to, nature offering its perfection, reminding you of your own. And yet other days it would frighten me. It became a hungry, lonely excuse for a sanctuary. Strange bird songs and chatter. Mysterious hideouts and unstable ground. Fungus, brittle dead leaves and thick logs that lay everywhere like severed limbs. My eyes were on its streams. My back on its moss. My stomach on its bark. My shadow became its nightfall and I tried to discover who I was there, to stare out the wild parts, to listen to the forest's voice echo back my own.

On the last night of the end of the world, we joined a gathering of two thousand people in the lungs of the rainforest, surrounded by the ruins of Mayan temples. We were at a crisis point; we all knew that. The ice caps were melting into the oceans and the oceans were rising; the gap between rich and poor was growing; urbanisation was slowly destroying the place we were all standing in. Calendars end and calendars begin, but time cannot be measured by starts and finishes. We knew that next year we'd still be breathing, that the world would still be intact. But there we were, alongside Nina, a teenager who had cycled all the way from Stockholm. Alongside Alan from Birmingham who'd swapped a stag do for naked hippies. We'd come together because we didn't want to carry on pretending we were helpless. We wanted to mark the start of the end.

The end came as a tropical storm; heavy rain made the pools of the rainforest overflow as passports and wallets were carried away downstream. Hundreds of us watched as our tiny dreams and huge ambitions were taken, our identities washed away. Nature was redefining us, she was telling us we were something worth finding again. So we sheltered in our tent like it was the end of the world, feeling a different kind of fear there; one of jaguars and scorpions and that we would have to give it all up too soon. That we might not make it back together in one piece. But we did. And we still are, intact beings with mouths full of stories just waiting to be told. I'll give myself to the forest now, to life. Just as it is, just as I am. And promise me you'll do the same. Just as it is, just as you are.

WE ARE BRAVER THIS WAY

How about a moment of silence for all those we have lost,
then a century of sound to replace them?
I'll talk you round till dusk and when the final countdown
comes we'll be dancing, won't we?
Our heads snapped back like elastic,
fingers clicking, waists twisting round to the start.
We'll put stopwatches next to our hearts and synchronise our breathing.
We'll be laughing, won't we?
Your eyes as dirty as mud piles,
gathering a memory for us to take on our way.
When the final countdown comes, we'll be counting along with it,
punching numbers out like boxers,
walking off into the darkness
finally brave enough to let go of one another at last.

Rebecca Tantony

Rebecca has performed poetry at the Royal Albert Hall, the Natural History Museum, The Barbican Theatre, The Royal Geographical Society and the Colston Hall, as well as a scattering of house parties and pub toilets. In 2012 she was awarded the Rising Stars Performance Poetry Award and spoke at the annual Mix Conference on the theme of Digital Media and Poetry. When not performing she teaches creative writing, working for various institutes and organisations including the globally-recognised creative writing centre, 826 Valencia. She is co-director of programmes for the Applied Theatre Action Initiative, an arts organisation that works with teenagers across the globe to create solution-focused social change. She has an intense love of black coffee, the Deep South of America and possess some exceptional dance moves.

Anna Higgie

Anna Higgie is an Australian born illustrator now living and working in Bristol, England. Anna spends most of her time in her Jamaica Street studio where she uses a combination of traditional and digital techniques to create her illustrations. After studying Painting and Fine Art at the National Art School in Sydney, Australia, Anna went on to study Illustration and Typography in London. She has since worked with a range of clients, including Penguin Books, Planet Mu Records, Bloomingdale's Department Store NYC, The Guardian and Varoom magazine, and has been a featured artist in Taschen's Illustration Now! series.

Lightning Source UK Ltd.
Milton Keynes UK
UKHW05f2130181018
330783UK00008B/128/P